The Mom Appreciation Book: A Creative Fill-In-The-Blank Venture The Perfect Gift for Mom

Mom,
My top 3 reasons you are
the best Mom ever:

1. ....

2. _____

3. ....

The heart of a mother is a deep abyss at the bottom of which you will always find forgiveness.

- Honore de Balzac

Mom,
You are my

_____

My mother had a great deal of trouble with me, but I think she enjoyed it.

-Nicholas Sparks

Mom,
I love how you

_____

_____

All that I am or ever hope to be,
I owe to my angel mother.

- Abraham Lincoln

Mom,
I really love it when

_____

_____

My mother was the most beautiful woman I ever saw.
All I am I owe to my mother.

- George Washington

Mom,
My favorite memory of us
from the past year was when

we _____

_____

_____

Life began with waking up and loving
my mother's face.

- George Eliot

Mom,
You always make me
laugh when you

_____

_____

I remember my mother's prayers and
they have always followed me.
They have clung to me all my life.

- Abraham Lincoln

Mom,
You always

_____

_____

_____

The best place to cry is a mother's arms.

- Jodi Picoult

Mom,
Thank you for

_____

_____

_____

_____

A mother is not a person to lean on,
but a person to make leaning unnecessary.

- Dorothy Canfield Fisher

Mom,
You make me

_____

_____

_____

There's no one way to be a perfect mother and million ways to be a good one.

- Jill Churchill

I am so _____

to be able to call you
my Mom

I realized when you look at your mother,
you are looking at the purest
love you will ever know.

- Mitch Albom

Mom,
I'll never forget when

_____

_____

_____

_____

Everybody wants to save the Earth;
nobody wants to help
Mom do the dishes.

- P.J. O'Rourke

Mom,
Thank you for instilling

_____

_____ in me.

Being a mother is an attitude, not a biological relation.

- Robert A. Heinlein

Mom,
Thanks for all the

_____

_____

_____

If evolution really works, how come mothers only have two hands?

- Milton Berle

Mom,
I will always love you
despite the fact you

_____

_____

To describe my mother would
be to write about a hurricane
in its perfect power. Or the climbing,
falling colors of a rainbow.

- Maya Angelou

Mom,
You make my day brighter
every time you

_____

_____

The phrase 'working mother' is redundant.

- Jane Sellman

Mom,
Without you I would

_____

_____

Youth fades; love droops; the leaves of friendship fall; A mother's secret hope outlives them all.

- Oliver Wendell Holmes

Mom,
Nobody can

_____

quite like you

33

Love as powerful as your mother's
for you leaves its own mark.
To have been loved so deeply will
give us some protection forever.

- J.R. Rowling

Mom,
I admire your

_____

_____

I tell my kids, 'I am thinking about you ever other minute of my day.'

- Michelle Obama

Mom,
Some people think you are
weird when you
_____, but I

know _____

A mother's arms are more
comforting than anyone else's.

- Princess Diana

Mom,
I look forward to

_____

_____

When you are a mother, you are never really alone in your thoughts. A mother always has to think twice, once for herself and once for her child.

- Sophia Loren

Mom,
I love watching

_____

_____ with you

Motherhood has a very humanizing effect. Everything gets reduced to essentials.

- Meryl Streep

Mom,
I love it when we talk about

_____

....

It's not easy being a mother.
If it were easy, fathers would do it.

- Dorothy

Mom,
I love that you always
_____ when
I'm having a bad day

Motherhood: All love begins
and ends there.

- Robert Browning

Mom,
You inspire me to be
a better person because

_____

_____

Acceptance, tolerance, bravery, compassion. These are the things my mom taught me.

- Lady Gaga

Mom,
You are not only my
_____, but also

my _____

49

As my mom always said, 'You'd rather have smile lines than frown lines.'

- Cindy Crawford

Mom,

Dad sometimes says that

you _____ , but I

_____

There were times when, in middle school and junior high, I didn't have a lot of friends. But my mom was always my friend. Always.

- Taylor Swift

Mom,
You always make me
laugh when you

You instantly become less selfish.
You can't be the biggest person
in the world anymore - they are.
Motherhood really grounds you.

- Keri Russell

Mom,

There is one more thing I've been meaning to tell you:

_____

_____

_____

There is no love like a mother's - she who carries the child that God knits in the womb, she who nourishes and guides, she who teaches and inspires, she who gives of her heart and soul and self for the good and the happiness of her children and her family.

-Ronald Reagan